ALAN McCREDIE is a professional photographer, fi
in photography at Edinburgh College. As well as hi
has published and collaborated on a number of bc ~ ~~~~~~~~~~~~.
Best known for his editorial and documentary work he has completed
several major projects to critical acclaim. He is a Perthshire man, now lost
to Leith.

Scotland the Braw

a celebration of all that is braw

Luath Press Limited

EDINBURGH

www.luath.co.uk

First published 2019

Reprinted 2020

ISBN: 978-1-913025-48-9

The paper used in this book is recyclable. It is made from
low chlorine pulps produced in a low energy, low
emission manner from renewable forests.

Printed and bound by Ashord Colour Press, Gosport

Typeset in 11 point Avenir Next

*This book is for my wife Jenny, my children Eilidh and Joe
and especially for my dad Norman,
all of whom are very definitely braw.*

braw

/braw/brah/

adjective SCOTTISH

Fine or fine-looking. Excellent.
"It was a braw summers day"

It happened every time – I'd be watching that perfect slice of Scandi-noir *The Bridge* and then the main character Saga would suddenly say 'bra' (she pronounced it braw) in an accent that seemed almost exactly the same as the one I used to hear growing up in Perth as a child – It made me laugh every time, and transported me straight back to the school playground. A lot of the kids from the country areas around Perth would often refer to things as 'braw'. I liked the word even then. It seemed kind and warm and had a good sound to it.

It's a fine word, 'braw'. It has that guttural Germanic roughness to it that always seems to make words just that bit heavier, as if they have been around for a good while (which braw certainly has) and become really grounded in the language.

Like so many other words, the roots of braw seem to lie somewhere on the Italian peninsula. It goes back to the Latin (don't they all…) and has since spread outwards. Its original meaning was brave and lives on as *bravo* in Italian and French. The root of both words, 'braw' and 'brave', is the

Latin *barbarus* and the Greek *barbaros*. By the late 16th century, it had spread north to Scotland and Scandinavia with the word becoming 'braw' and 'bra' respectively, and its meaning has changed to 'fine', 'good' or 'pleasing'.

An alternative title for this book could be Scotland the Brave, or much more interestingly Scotland the Barbarous (maybe that will be the next one…).

So, yes, Scotland, and indeed every other country on the planet, is braw. Braw can be the sun setting after a perfect day, it can be a state of mind, it can be an umbrella blown away during a storm, a red rubber ball, the sound of distant church bells on a cold winter's morning. It's good to have a sense of wonder about the country you live in but I would say it is even more important to be able to laugh at all a country's foibles and idiosyncrasies. It's the flaws that always make things more interesting.

Scotland, again like all other countries, is braw in a myriad of different ways. Some see Scotland as a place of rugged Highland vistas, some see the post-industrial sadness that is a testament to the land that was. Some say it is the people that make a country, others say it is the culture and the history. All of these ingredients are important but they are far more potent when they are mixed together than they ever could be in isolation.

My previous book *Scotland the Dreich* was logistically somewhat harder than this one. Believe it or not, it doesn't always rain in Scotland and there were days when I would set off from a dreich Edinburgh only to find blue skies over Glencoe. I must have been the only person in the country praying for a day of dismal gloom. No such issues with this book though as 'brawness' has many faces and essentially if it made me laugh, if it made me smile or if it made me think 'Oh, that's lovely' then it made it in.

What a delight to roam the countryside of Scotland! Taking the unplanned road has always been one of the greatest pleasures for me and many a dead end and winding country road was driven down in the making of this little book. I believe it is the small things that really make up the character of a nation. The chest-beating and flag-waving has never really been for me – I've just never felt the need to show my appreciation of Scotland in such a way. To sit on a deserted beach looking out over the Atlantic Ocean as the sun slowly sinks, or to pick slowly around abandoned places where the sense of history is overwhelming are where I find the truth of places and get a sense of what a country feels like.

The photographs in this book were taken over the last couple of years, with the vast majority being taken between January and July 2019. To always have a camera handy is essential in a book like this, for although some images can be planned in advance, it is the unexpected moments that so often make the best photographs (who could foresee a peacock at a window?). I set out with no particular angle in mind and just let the book go its own way. My only proviso was to be positive. Every image in the book is, to me, a celebration of the countryside and the people. If it was braw it made it in; if it wasn't, it didn't.

Scotland the Braw is about Scotland, but it could just as easily be about anywhere else. All countries and places have their wonders and all are exceptional in their own varied and differing ways. All contribute equally to life's rich pageant and in such fractious times as these, I think it is even more important to remember that we really are all in this together.

Be braw!

Acknowledgements

In helping to make this book I would like to say a big thank you to
The Canny Man's pub in Edinburgh, Scottish Power, Pitlochry Highland
Games and especially to Val McDermid and Prof Jo Sharp
for their constant and kind support.

I Am Exactly Where I Used To Be

Up and over the soft hills where the grass is cut shorter than the green on a golf course and suddenly the golden sands and turquoise bay appear. Homer would be at home here, but instead Ossian is the one who stalks these far shores.

A Memory of Youthful Sundays

With its watchtowers built with a nod to the Romantic ideal of the Rhine valley, Scotland's mightiest river, the Tay, oscillates wildly through the fertile fruit lands of the Carse of Gowrie, on towards the distant sea and the wonders of exotic ports, like Dundee.

The Ballad of Penny Falls and the One-Armed Bandit

It's all colour and noise, noise and colour. The penny falls are now ten pence a go and the one-armed bandits have lost their solitary limb. Still the wheels turn and the cherries pop and the silvery coins crash into the metal tray, to be scooped up and used again. Never has the sound of money sounded quite so brash, and quite so good.

Ships Will Wake to the Sound of Church Bells

We'd spent the day picking through the headstones of my ancestors in the overgrown cemetery at Logierait before, like homesick amphibians, we headed to the river. There, on an antique bridge over the River Tummel we watched as, for seconds only, we travelled back in time to an era when little red roadsters ruled the land.

In Search of Snow Covered Croci

It came from the East. All bestial and snarling. It shut schools and businesses, reduced roads to cresta runs and delighted a million children with days of snow. On Leith Links, skis became the chosen method of transport and for three glorious days the world seemed to pause, hold its breath and quietly wait.

Safe Harbour, on Rougher Seas

We round the corner and there over the brow of the hill lies as pleasing a sight as there ever was. A small town, folded up like the moraine from an ancient glacier, hugs the contours of the land and seems to belong here, and nowhere else. Hotels, bars, amusement arcades, boats and cafes all thrive but the BIG CHURCH overlooks them all with a stern 'steady now' in case the frivolity becomes too much.

Up There the Winds are Ferocious

Scotland is so often a victim of the weather, but when the weather-gods smile down upon us, my word don't we take full advantage of it. In Pitlochry, in the heart of Perthshire, the Highland Games are in full swing and amidst whisky, shortbread, picnics and music, the BIG MEN of the heavy events take centre stage and whirl their hammers and toss their cabers with seemingly no thought to the consequences...

The Chaotic Passing of Time

Is there a finer existence than to be on an empty beach, in the early summer sunshine, looking west to the blue Isle of Skye? The only sound is the whooping of the gulls, the murmur of the sea and the putt-putt of a far fishing boat. My dog certainly thought so, although I had guilty yearnings for busy city-centre bars...

An Uncertain Smile

The kilted barbarians stalk the gift shops of Edinburgh's Royal Mile. Once it was the Roman tourists who tried to conquer then assimilate the wild tribes from beyond the walls, now the eternal tourist lays siege to the nation. They are always very welcome and even more so when they wear skirts of such a fetching cut.

A Short Visit to Elyssian Fields

The sun's out. It's Scotland. QUICK – GET THE SUN TAN LOTION OUT!!!
And who needs a beach when there are the tranquil meadows of the
central reservation of a dual carriageway to transport you to Monaco,
where the white van men are replaced by Grand Prix racing drivers.

This is the Water, and This is the Well

The UK's smallest commercial radio station, Two Lochs Radio, broadcasts from the village of Gairloch in Wester Ross to the hills, glens, homes, beaches, lochs and mountains of the area. From *A Rock & Roll Saturday* all through the *Celtic Weekend,* the volunteers who run the station keep the music alive, and show why, a century on, radio will always kill the video star.

A Seemingly Unconnected Event

In Scotland, we dress for dinner. Full Highland dress is mandatory for fish suppers in the street and these are the laws our fathers and mothers passed down to us. In the west, our sporrans bulge with vinegar; in Edinburgh and the east, it is brown chippy sauce we tuck away in our badger skin pouches. In Perth, it is all tartan trousers and mayonnaise.

Of Spirits and Wild Horses

I'd grown weary of the long, straight road arrowing through the flat and smoky peatland between Port Ellen and Bowmore. To leave the familiar way and head off down a route never travelled before is always a joy. My reward stood patiently waiting at a turn in the road. The two horses could have been quietly standing there since the beginning of time. A moment of stillness and a moment of quiet, before they trotted off and the sun fell behind the horizon.

An Unexplained Atmosphere of Panic

It's as good a word as any to put on the front of a building. It reminds me of how I used to love the fronts of buildings until I realised it was all just a facade.

Sitting quietly in la belle Perth, this building was an auctioneers until recently and according to the Registers of Scotland is now at risk.

A Glance Inward, to Mystery

Some run marathons, others scale the heights of tall mountains and there are those who throw themselves off high buildings with nothing but a bit of silk to check their descent.

And then there are those true adventurers, the real thrill seekers, who quietly, doggedly and heroically munch, bite and sook their way through an entire wall of boiled sweets. For me though, a cinnamon ball is all I need.

Only When We Build, Do We Know What We Need

The black dam of Loch Sloy, high in the hills to the west of Loch Lomond, sits brooding, almost waiting for the armies of Mordor to spew forth from its water gates. This was the first hydro-electric scheme to be built in Scotland and it began powering the grid in 1950. It stands impressive and solid, a testament to those who built it and the 21 men who died during its construction.

Casting the Spell of Height Upon the Young

They look all cuddly, woolly and docile, but don't walk alone at night in these parts for that is when the sheep, ghostly and silent, stalk the lonely roads in search of their prey. Many a weary traveller has set out, never to return, taken by the 'devil clouds' that roam these hills.

BEWARE OF SHEEP

How to Lose The Body, and Discover Flight

On the far north-west coast of Scotland, at the height of summer, the darkness never fully takes hold. To pitch a solitary tent by a remote beach with only the calling of the curlews and the herring gulls for company is one of the true pleasures of being alive. Look to the west before sleep, and wonder.

Night Life During Wartime

Every Saturday, the buses criss-cross the country taking that most hopeful of person, the football fan, to faraway towns and unfamiliar pies, in supplication to their team. The sun shines as they leave, but will the return journey be fair or stormy?

A Tumble of Hills to Deceive The Eye

In this unchanging and forever moving landscape, the clouds whip noisily and chaotically through a rain-heavy sky. Vast shapes loom in the distance – their form only to be guessed at as they brood, imagined only, in their lair.

For a moment, the clouds thin and what was once iron-dark is suddenly etched with the finest silver filigree. But only for a moment – a blink and the magic fades, only to be half remembered, like a teenage dream.

Yesterday Waits In Ribbons

Oh! Isn't that a pretty sun, sitting in a pretty sky! We stayed to watch it darken as an evening tide sucked the sand and the last warmth of the day from beneath our feet.

And tomorrow we do the same thing all over again.

Those Threatening Ships Were Not Pirates After All

The sun is still well below the horizon, but high above in the cold stratosphere something is happening. Ice crystals have formed and reflect the light from the still hidden sun back down to Earth. Rare and fleeting, these pearlescent, nacreous clouds are a wonder seldom seen, and turn a bitterly cold winter morning into a small glimpse of whatever heaven you may choose to believe in.

Driving Without Maps

First there was the red rail bridge, serpentining over the river, which sat alone for 70 or so years before a younger sibling arrived with a swoop of gunmetal grey, carrying an army of vehicles north to the mountains and glens. A third arrived, section by section, completing a trilogy of crossings, each one built in a different century, but united in their need to ensure the movement of the people.

The World Pauses, Looks Around, and Wanders Off

TWAT!

The lower leagues of Scottish football are no place for the faint-hearted where sticks and stones may not break your bones, but the thunderous tackles most certainly will. On a pitch, heavy with Borders rain, the mud soon sucks the marrow out of bones and a mug of glucose energy drink, is manna for the soul.

To the Land Where the Rivers Freely Flow

In the city of the dead, the barely alive are kings, and so it is on this cold morning. Like a screenshot from every young goth's dream, the Necropolis in Glasgow is a monument to what has been and what will one day be.

The Morning Is Afraid of Going Back to Sleep

This is Mull. This is Tobermory. This is lunchtime. This is the busy cafe with no seats inside. This is alfresco dining. This is Scotland.

This is Midsummer's Day.

The Traveller Haunts Strange and Far Places

Built in 1748, yet strangely not lit until 1800 (they couldn't find the matches), the old lighthouse at Southerness is the second oldest in Scotland. It stands sentinel over the Solway Firth where once ships ploughed to and fro between Dumfries and the wide world, and John Paul Jones switched his allegiances and became an American hero.

It once shone its light down to the far hills of the Lake District to the south but it last shone its light in 1936 and is unlikely to ever to do so again.

A Time Before Words

The Paps of Jura sit proudly on Orwell's island of *Nineteen Eighty-Four* fame. He sat, years ago now, ill and dying, clattering away on his typewriter and seeing a vision of the future sadly not as far-fetched now as it may have seemed to him at the time.

The Sounds of Far-away Trains

If you stop, stand silently and listen, you can almost hear them. Yesterday's trains, far away now, have left something behind. The whistles, clamour and clanking seem to clatter in on the wind while, just out of earshot, the shuffle of a million waiting passengers.

The trains long ago abandoned this place but here it stands, like me, quietly listening. And waiting.

When All Else Fails, Head Downhill

A quiet bar, empty barstools and a selection of drinks that would take a very large chunk of time to get through. As pleasant a sight as could be hoped for, and a sight that in some cases, such as here, has changed very little over decades.

It would be tremendously rude, an act of historical barbarism, to leave without occupying a soft stool at a long bar.

Tall Buildings on Small Islands

I hadn't come to Islay for the whisky (too much peat for my palate) but Islay is made of whisky and, like London and its rodents, you are never that far away from a distillery or three. And of them all this is my favourite – again not for the drink, I'm too unsophisticated for that, but for the whitewashed building, the brick chimney and the red of the post box that seem in perfect harmony to me.

Portrait Of Earth, from A Car Window

If you've missed the postman, there is always the postsheep. Fasten your letter to its fleece and sit back and relax in the knowledge that your package will be delivered safe and sound. However, it may take a while and there is a distinct possibility it will be gnawed at on the way.

Just Because You Feel At Ease, the Danger Is Not Always Over

Once upon a time, the motorist was an adventurer, roaring along narrow roads, as wider ones had yet to be built. On those long and lonely ways through the north and west of Scotland, fuel was always an issue. A network of small rural filling stations shot up and still, even today, we can trace the line from then to now.

Imagine puttering over the crest of a hill, dangerously low on petrol, and finding one of these oases of petroleum, lying quietly in the gloom like a habitable planet in a far away solar system.

What We See Underwater, Is More Clear Than What We See Through Air

Who would have known that tucked away beside a hillside track, the summer pools of our youth still exist? Here they are – dappled by sunlight and gently buzzed by bees. The cool water refreshes the hot and the dusty and allows harbours to be built, pooh sticks to be played and tiddlers to be watched.

And Now It Is the Middle of the Summer Moon

Egypt may have its Pyramids, Tibet its mountains, Dubai its garish towers of bling but they all fade into insignificance when faced with the mighty presence of – yes, truly – the world's largest hedge. Surely the greatest achievement in all of Scotland? For the Meikleour Beech Hedge is all that and more. Wonder at its height! Marvel at its girth!

Spare a thought for the size of the hedge trimmer to keep it in tip top condition.

How Do We Get Back Home?

The old gods are out tonight, and the May Queen is here to welcome them. It is Beltane, the Celtic celebration that marks the beginning of summer. As the sun's fire diminishes in the west, the bonfires are lit and the pagan night comes alive in a celebration that has echoed though the ages and that brings us here, in this place, at this time.

Set Sail for Bluer Skies!

It sits, hugely impressive at the far wall. It seems to be made of the same material and designed by the same people as the rocket ships in the old Flash Gordon series from the 1930s. Would Ming the Merciless be so foolish as to attack this treasure craft though, laden as it is with the battered jewels of Fife? I worry that he might, so help liberate some of those deep-fried wonders as any sane person would.

CASH SALES
ONLY.

Not All Aspirin Alike

I sat looking at the sign for a while. And yet there were no lobsters to be found.

A crustacean frustration...

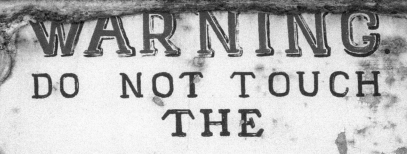

The Future Ain't What It Used to Be

Although I did not feel like a mince round, I skipped into the shop nonetheless and the pieman did cometh. I asked why the James Hogg Shepherds Pie was famous and was told that only those who need to know would ask that. I bought a Scotch Pie and left, strangely bereft at the gap in my pastry-based knowledge.

Pork Pie with Black Pud
Cranberry & Port Topping
New £2.60

PORK PIE with
STILTON & BRIE
TOPPING £2.80

Homemade
Pork, Brussel and
Cheddar Crunchies £1.50

Big 'N' Beefy
Beef Steak & Gravy
Bakes £2.00

Big 'N' Beefy
Steak,Cheese & Chilli
Bakes £2.00

Venison & Haggis Roll
Made with our Special
Haggis £2.80

Haggis,Potato
Carrot & Turnip
Pie £1.50

Homemade
Pork,Stilton and Garlic
Crunchies £1.50

Homemade
Pork Sausage Rolls
£1.50 Each

amous
Hogg
Pie 2.50

Beef Steak
Ale & Stilton Pie
Feeds 2 £5.40

Large Beef Mince
Round Pie
£3.00

Chicken,Ham
and Mushroom pie
feeds 2-3 £3.00

Homemade
Beef Steak Pie
£7.00

Hom
Beef Steak
Pie

Wild Boar and Venison
Game Pie
£5.80 feeds 7

Medium Sized
Beef Steak Pie
Feeds 2 £5.40

Large Chicken
Round Pie
Feeds 2-3 £3.00

Homemade
Beef Steak & Kidney
Pies, lge £5, Ind £2

A Hundred Years of Sheep

It's the main route west between Stirling and Loch Lomond and on to the happy isles of the west coast. But no harassed salesperson, no ambling tourist motor-home or day-tripper takes precedence over the locals, who wind their merry way from field to field where the grass really is sometimes greener.

At Rainbow's End

With 5p in our pockets, we used to haunt these places. These palaces. It maybe doesn't buy so much in our adulthood as it once did but the memory of our youth remains and the clenched fist, with the coin making an imprint on your skin, is as vibrant now as it once was. I'll have two fruit salads and three blackjacks please.

Do Not Fear the Dark Waters

It sits suspended between the trees, like the high road between two sylvan kingdoms. A slow highland river passes below and I wonder where this bridge leads and where it comes from. Like all bridges, it completes the path and leaps over gaps. And like all bridges it demands to be crossed.

The Centre Must Hold

For a country as asymmetrical as Scotland, we have our fair share of places that lay claim to the centre of the land. Most are on godforsaken stretches of bleak moor, marked by nothing other than a bitter wind and a cold rain. This one, with no more claim than any of the others, is my favourite though. It at least has the sense of pride to actually mark with a cross (etched somewhat haphazardly into the centre stone) the supposed centre of Scotland.

Is it the centre of Scotland? Almost certainly not, but anywhere where X marks that spot deserves some form of recognition.

To Stare at Seas Long Gone

Some say it follows the line of the rocks as they lead out to sea. Some say it is ergonomically designed to break the water as best it can. Some say it mirrors the stars of a particularly distant and unloved constellation. But who says it was built by a drunken shoal of fishermen, zigzagging their way, late one Friday night in 1879? I say it was, and mine is the best explanation of them all.

You Don't Need a Weatherman to Know Which Way the Wind Blows

I'd seen the tree all week from the coast road where a holiday had taken us. It was at the top of a sloping field that was always full of cows and more worryingly an evil-looking bull. On our last day, the field was empty and I took my chance. Only it wasn't entirely empty... A few grumpy sheep didn't like me being there and I had only a few minutes to get through the field, get my shot and run. And I did run – those sheep had fearsome-looking horns and a butting was definitely in the offing.

The Light that Falls on Faraway Shores

It's been decades since the old lighthouse at Newhaven harbour last shone, but if on a moonlit night you choose your moment, work out your angles, and brave the seaweed-slippy slipway then you will be rewarded, for a moment, with a glimpse of what used to be.

A Voyage to the Interior

I like the derelict places, the forgotten places, the ugly places – the places that used to be something and now stand witness to the passing of time, and the passing of their own importance.

All of this was useless at Loch Katrine – the place is so ridiculously picturesque that my search for gritty post-industrialist images was in vain. Thwarted, I was forced to take a cruise up the loch in a century-old steamship, drinking tea in the sun, and watching a landscape of unrivalled beauty glide slowly past.

If you visit here, I guarantee it will seize you by the Trossachs.

The Stones Honour the Dead, the Sand Honours the Living

We'd been tracking them for days. High up in the bleak country of Sherrifmuir, we found clues to their movements. The red-haired Scotch have definitely passed this way, and like an offering, have left their russet locks to prove it, tangled on some old barbed wire.

Let the Bright One In

Tap tap at the window.

Danny Glick, who by clawing at windows in Salem's Lot haunted my childhood, comes instantly to mind. This garish brute is no less scary as he clearly has his beady eye on my breakfast. 'I am dressed far better than you are', he seems to be saying, which I cannot disagree with.

I have better legs though.

Soon There Will Be No One Left to Remember

All hail the riders!!!

They have ridden through rivers, crossed fields and rode the high ridges and finally they descend from Venchen Hill over the Bowmont Water to Town Yetholm, where they will dismount. The Kelso Laddie will meet with the Bari Manushi and the Bari Gadgi and, as evening falls, the Riders of the Marches will disperse as the Borders night takes back its history.

For those that are interested in such things, I used four cameras in the making of this book. My old and trusty Nikon D700 and D800 did the bulk of the work and these cameras have served me very well as a professional photographer over the last decade.

I usually keep a smaller camera with me, in a bag or in the car, for those unexpected moments that occur more frequently than you would think. For this I use my Fuji X100 camera. A lovely little camera that actually makes you want to use it, such is the beauty of its design.

And don't forget the humble iPhone. There are a couple of images in this book that were taken with my phone. Phone photography is improving year by year and this is the real growth area of photography – it's a hugely exciting area and one that I am sure will deliver great things in the next few years. Never be afraid of change.

Achmelvich Beach, north of Lochinver

Tarbert, Kintyre

Kinnoull Hill, Perth, looking east over the Carse of Gowrie

Pitlochry, Perthshire

Largs, Ayrshire

Big Sand, near Gairloch in Wester Ross

The old bridge over the River Tummel, Logierait, Perthshire

The Royal Mile, Edinburgh

Leith Links, Leith, Edinburgh

Greenock

Gairloch, Wester Ross

Loch Sloy

North Berwick

Somewhere near Morebattle in the Scottish Borders

Somewhere in the middle of Islay

Wild camping, near Kinlochbervie in Sutherland

Perth

Somewhere between Edinburgh and Ayr

Pittenweem

Beyond the Fairy Pools, Skye

 Musselburgh, East Lothian

 Early morning,
near Ullapool

 Queensferry Crossing

 Hawick, Scottish Borders

 The Necropolis, Glasgow

 Tobermory, Isle of Mull

 Southerness, Dumfries &
Galloway

 Paps of Jura, Jura

 Riccarton Junction, Wauchope
Forest, Scottish Borders

 The Canny Man's, Edinburgh

Lagavulin, Islay

Beltane, Calton Hill, Edinburgh

On the road to Red Point, Wester Ross

Pittenweem

Tarbert, Kintyre

Crail, East Neuk of Fife

Craigrockall Burn, Criffel, Kirkcudbrightshire

Butchers, anywhere in Scotland... (although it's actually Melrose)

Meikleour Beech Hedge, Perthshire

Arnprior, Stirlingshire

 Edinburgh Corner Shop

 Newhaven Harbour, Edinburgh

River crossing, somewhere west of Blair Atholl

 Loch Katrine

 The alleged centre of Scotland, near Newtonmore

 Sherrifmuir

 St Monans Harbour

 The lair of the peacock

 Carrick Bay, Dumfries and Galloway

 Yetholm, Scottish Borders

Scotland the Dreich

Alan McCredie

ISBN: 978-1-910745-82-3 PBK £7.99

This book is a celebration of all that is dreich. To my mind the images in this book are uplifting and joyful. There is nothing miserable about dreich. A sunny day has no more right to exist than a dreich one. Here, then, are fifty dreich images, accompanied by 50 equally dreich captions.

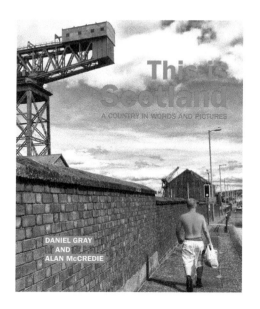

This Is Scotland

Daniel Gray & Alan McCredie

ISBN: 978-1-910021-59-0 PBK £9.99

A Scotsman and an Englishman, a camera and a notebook. The pictures tell a thousand stories, the words tell the time. This is Scotland, captured at its most crucial point for 300 years. United by a love of Scotland, warts and all. Especially its warts, in fact. Gray and McCredie set out on a journey high and low, mainland and island, rust and heather, to document a country and its people. Here is a country caught and sketched before it disappears, one of flaking pub signs and tenant crofters, Italian cafes and proper fitba' grounds. Stunning and moving images are coupled with lyrical and nostalgic prose to make a work which will become a reference point, a Caledonian comfort, an antidote to shortbread-tin Scotland.

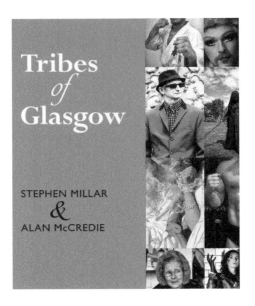

Tribes of Glasgow

Stephen Millar & Alan McCredie

ISBN: 978-1-912147-85-4 PBK £14.99

Stephen Millar and Alan McCredie took to the streets of Scotland's largest city to depict the multitude of groups, both old and modern, that make up its population. From cowboys to cosplayers, Barras traders to bikers, and gunslingers to goths, forget *Humans of New York* – these are the *Tribes of Glasgow*.